A Poetic Journey To Love

A Brief Look At The Stages of Love

Everett R. Callaway

Copyright © 2016 Everett Callaway

All rights reserved!
Unlawful duplication and/or distribution of this book is prohibited!

Self-Published via Blurb in Nashville, TN

Distributed by Ingram Content Group

ISBN 9781367837782

Acknowledgments:

There are so many people who I would like to say thank you to for always being supportive of my endeavors. Several family members and friends have been instrumental in what modicum of success and achievements I have realized in my life. I would, however, like to highlight some very special people:

Thank you:

To my mom: Mary J. Mckinnon (Clark)

I could sit at this computer and type from now until Jesus returns and not comprehensively encapsulate what you meant to me in your physical life and what you continue to mean to me in your spiritual one. I hope to thank you again when our spirits commune in Heaven!

To my wife: Christina Callaway

No one has ever demanded more from me than you. Your never ending pursuit of righteousness and achievement are unparalleled in my life. I regret it took me as long as it did to truly understand and appreciate it. Thank you for maintaining a gaze and heart affixed upon God. Thank you for loving and supporting me.

To my God/Savior: Jesus Christ

Heavenly Father! All the things I am thankful for are because of you. Thank you for the Love (John 3:16)! Thank you for the admonition (Matt.6:33)! I pray that if there is any good that I do, you, and you alone, will get the glory!

A Poetic Journey To Love

Table of Contents

Introduction   page 2
I.   The Pain of Love's Game   page 3
II.   Love Unknown   page 6
III.   The Chase   page 9
IV.   Does He?   page 13
V.   Friendship: The Flower of Love   page 16
VI.   Soul Mates   page 19
VII.   Appreciate   page 22
VIII. You, Me & Unity   page 25
IX.   I Want To Live (Love of Self)   page 28
X.   Dead Beat Dad (Love our Kids)   page 33
XI.   Hey Mom (A Motherly Love)   page 36
XII.   Can You Forgive Me? (Agape Love)   page 43

Introduction

It is said that *Love* is the universal language. It can be defined as having deep affection for something or someone, involving intense feelings. The word 'love' has been thrown around haphazardly nowadays to identify an affinity for a favorite food, song or movie star. But, love, in its purest sense, is best represented when associated with affairs of the heart.

We all, at one point or another, have longed for love, been in love, or, have loved and lost. *A Poetic Journey To Love* attempts to encapsulate all the feelings experienced on love's journey, at every stage. Will you and your companion smile when you reminisce over who pursued whom back in the beginning? Or, will your eyes be opened if you are currently in a loveless relationship?

No matter where you are on your personal odyssey of love, there is sure to be something anecdotally, within this book, to remind you where you've been, clarify where you are, or, prepare you for where you're headed...in love!

Chapter 1

The Pain of Love's Game

Who knew, who knows....who will ever know,
How it hurts inside, the torture's slow-
What is out is not in, I just don't reveal,
Empty is the heart, craving a refill-
Outside I laugh, while inside I cry,
Outside I live, while inside...I die-
What unseen force revels in my pain,
Is my misfortune the subject of a game-
Some puppet-master exposing my thoughts,
Show love, take love....exploiting my faults-
Is the most worthy unworthy of God's greatest Gift,
Like sand in that glass, my faith does sift-
You see, the love that made me now evades me,
Could it be, maybe, that even LOVE hates me-
Or, is Cupid just derelict in his duties,
Of providing me with love like found in the movies-
Still, my plan is to expand my threshold of pain,
For, I plan to withstand while playing...Love's Game!

Few may acknowledge or admit it, but, this is a stage many people have had to navigate. You patiently or, maybe, impatiently await the arrival of 'the one'. Sometimes it's one failed attempt after another, to the point where you sour on even wanting to meet anyone. Frustration mounts and you begin to even question God about His plans for that special someone in your life.

Some pretend to be perfectly content being single. They display no outward sign of longing or emptiness. However, love, in some form or fashion is needed, just like the air we breathe. Although it is a slower death than lacking oxygen, it is still a death.

In efforts to mask the pain associated with a life devoid of love, people will immerse themselves in their careers or jobs. Or, some will turn to the party scene and pretend to never be a 'one woman' or 'one man' person. But, at the beginning, middle and end of the day, everybody needs love.

A sad state is when you have those individuals that dip in and out of relationships in search of that feeling. They enter into a relationship they shouldn't venture into, and stay in one they should get out of!

My personal belief is that when you focus on you, then, love will find you! One must acquire a level of self-contentment and self-love, first. We should prepare for someone to complement, or, add to what has already been established internally and not for someone to bring you the happiness or feelings of appreciation that you desire.

Do you remember when you were at this stage….or, are you there now?

Chapter II

Love Unknown

How does it feel to not know,
That you have total control over my soul-
Then, again, how could you not know,
When the look in my eyes should say so-
First, you hooked me with your smile,
Then, you reeled me in with your style-
But, I didn't resist, I came willingly,
And, not knowing your kiss is just killing me-
How do you go about your day so nonchalantly,
When all I want out of life is you to want me-
Goose bumps tell me you are different,
And, for me to go there is real significant-
How do you love someone you don't even know,
Where do you hide a love you can't even show-
Guess, I'll continue our love on my own,
And, this will forever remain a LOVE UNKNOWN!

At some point in our lives, we have all seen that person from afar that piques our interest just a bit more than the rest. I mean, sure, there is a physical attraction, however, there seems to be something just a tad bit more special about this person. Is it that person that you seem to bump into frequently at the market? Or, that co-worker in another department that has you entering and leaving the building most approximate to their desk, even though you work on the other side of the building? No matter who that person is for you, it seems to be impossible to not think about him or her.

On this stage of the journey, there's a lot of daydreaming. There is a lot of wondering "what if"? You visualize yourself and that person whitewater kayaking. How about the two of you on a cruise ship sailing the Mediterranean? Here you are with all these visions of ecstasy dancing around in your head, and you haven't as much as said good morning to this person. If there are any moments of eyes meeting, you quickly look away to avoid any detection in your eyes that might expose you.

Does this person even know you exist? How amazing it is for one person to long for and desire another, and, for the desired individual to not know the 'desirer' exists. Or, is it worse for the desired person to know that you do exist?

What about that friend or co-worker that you are in proximity to on a daily basis? You know, the one who confides in you about everything happening, good or bad, in a current relationship. Speaking up about your feelings could ruin a good relationship, so, you bite your tongue and keep those feelings bottled up inside!

Do you remember when you felt like this about someone….or, maybe you're there right now?

Chapter III

The Chase

You flee the crime scene, although you're the victim,
You're the best I've seen, such beauty and wisdom-
So, I give chase, but, you continue to flee,
Is it me that you flee, or, simply flee to be free-
But, I offer no pressure, just love you can treasure,
Pure passion and pleasure, that no ruler can measure-

I chase you not to harass you, or to arrest you,
But, to caress you; forget what the rest do,
Come see what the best do-
Not to contain you, nor to detain you,
Or to restrain you, that's what the insane do-
Instead, I would court you, love and support you,
Write millions of love letters for you to sort through-

(cont.)

*Respecting your space, I'll maintain my distance,
But, will persist to pursue at my heart's insistence-
In your rear-view mirror, you'll see I'm behind you,
No matter how fast you flee, my heart will find you-
My want is to catch you, but, not to entrap you,
Put an end to this chase, so, then, I can wrap you-
In these real strong arms to forever protect you,
But, should you still want to flee, as your friend...
...I would let you!*

Many times, when we meet someone we are interested in, they are either in, or, recently out of a serious relationship. Oftentimes, an individual could be on the precipice of leaving an unfruitful situation and not quite ready, mentally, to engage in another. Someone running from one relationship can be reticent, or timid, about running into another.

One of the biggest challenges people in this circumstance (the chaser) will face is tightrope-walking between being supportive and understanding, while, also being reassuring that they are different. It is quite possible that he or she (the chased) heard similar sentiments from the previous companion. Being overly aggressive in pursuit can definitely be seen as an attempt to prey upon someone's vulnerabilities, or taking advantage.

As will be illustrated (hopefully) in an upcoming chapter, establishing a true, ulterior-motiveless friendship is paramount in gaining trust. When we truly care for or about someone, we must want what is best for that person, whether it includes us or not.

I know that is not groundbreaking information, however, this is a misstep that occurs frequently during this stage of a journey to love!

Are you chasing someone right now? Or, maybe there is someone chasing after you!

Chapter IV

Does He?

Does he hug you like he did on your first date?
Does he treat your sweet lips like a succulent grape?
Does he look into your eyes to see your desires?
Does he still have what it takes to light your fires?
Does he take you out at night, does he still hold your hand?
Does he change around friends, does he try to grandstand?
Does he pull out your chair when you're out for the evening?
Does he know why you're crying or care if you're grieving?
Does he show love to your kids, an extension of you?
When he speaks to other women, is he mentioning you?
Does he make love to your mind, spirit, body and soul?
Does he plan to be your man until you both grow old?
All these things for you, does he do, be for real?
'Cause, if he doesn't, then, he should...but, if he won't, I Will!

Ok, forget what I said last chapter! Well, maybe not all of it. But, look, sometimes you just gotta bring it. So, your person of interest is still hemming and hawing about how things were not really that bad in a previous/current relationship. She may attempt to rationalize things by saying "well, he only cheated on me because he has been hurt before, and, now he is afraid of commitment!" Or, he may postulate "….and, maybe going out every weekend with her girls is just a way of coping with stress!"

Sometimes, you just have to be bold and speak up. Sometimes you just have to give that person a reality check. Too many people get comfortable with the status quo in a relationship thinking it's better to play it safe. Again, strangely enough, some try to rationalize, or make excuses, in defense of their 'loved' ones that are mistreating them.

I recently saw a Facebook post where this guy made a video addressing another male who he knows is having an affair with his girlfriend. In this video, he tells the other guy he's not upset that he is involved with his girlfriend, but, that he's upset with how poorly the guy is executing his role as the 'side dude.'

After giving a tutorial about how to go about cheating with his girl and not getting caught, he finishes his tirade by saying he knows that viewers won't understand, but, when you love someone these are the measures you undertake. Wait,..what?

Nevertheless, your role in this stage of love's journey may be to give a wake-up call to your love interest. This should be done in a loving, caring and selfless manner, of course. A honest and sincere juxtaposition of how that person is being treated versus how they deserve to be treated may be the doctor's order.

Are you in need of a reality check….right now?

Chapter V

Friendship: the flower of love

Like sunshine, falling rain, blue skies,
Your style, smile, warmth, your eyes-
Are the elements to the flower of my soul,
However, minus friendship, my love won't grow-
Like a seed is what you need to start the process,
Trust is a must, without it, no progress-
Play games, no gain, I can't participate,
I can't, like a plant, you must communicate-
With me; for me to thrive, it's essential,
So our friendship can reach its fullest potential-
Too much deceit, like water, can drown me,
Be a safe place, like a vase, and surround me-
Relationships built on friendship are awesome,
And, sometimes even true love will blossom!!!

So, in this particular stage of love, interest may or may not have been expressed. If you reached this level via the aforementioned route of a reality check, then, this stage may prove a bit more challenging. You have expressed an interest in someone, so, he or she may be somewhat circumspect of your intentions when trying to establish a friendship. It is still possible, but, will require more effort. However, if you bypassed the previous stage and are focused on solidifying yourself as worthy of another's trust, then, that is exactly what should be done.

True friendship is congruent with truly having someone's best interest at heart. Even, if this genuine caring puts the friendship at risk, it is paramount that this sincerity is evident. Although there may be a strong attraction for the other party, true friendship may mean accepting that you are not what is best for that person. True friendship may mean that you offer advice sans the slant toward your ulterior motive. The poem intimates that in order for the flower of love to sprout, the seed of trust must first be planted.

As children of God, we are called to love one another. We should love each other regardless of circumstances. However, I find it more challenging to like some people versus loving them. I feel that we love each other because God commands us to, but, we like others because we choose to. Succinctly, we may love someone for who they are (child of God), but, not like them for how they are! Making sure that we are not caught up in the flowery emotions and the idea of being in love with someone, before actually ensuring that we like that person, could prove beneficial in the success of a relationship.

Time should truly be taken to investigate our motives when establishing a friendship. Do we really have the other person's best interest at heart, or, are our intentions only self-serving? If an intimate relationship is not in the books, can a platonic relationship survive? For, within the confines of an intimate relationship, when things go left, it is the foundation of friendship (caring, supporting, liking) that will be the life-preserver to save you from the abyss that many relationships fall into!

What are you right now…friend or foe?

Chapter VI

Soul mates?

I know what it takes to get you, it's gonna take to keep you,
I planted a seed of love, girl, with hopes that I would reap you-
I need you, to need me, to need you,
May I lead you from pain, like Moses did the Hebrew-
If hungry for love, girl, please, may I feed you,
You're so deep in my heart, love, if cut I would bleed you-
Can we send our souls together on a date,
To see if they're each other's human mate-
I will croon a love tune while our souls commune,
Strawberries with wine is what we'll consume-
See, I've fallen for you, girl, and I don't wanna get up,
You're that coffee pot of love, boo, that fills my cup-
And, when our souls return to confirm what I yearn,
Then, never again will you have a concern-
For, on the wings of love, I'll be happy to carry thee,
And, all that's left for me to do is ask you to marry me!

Finally, you've made it! This is the stage that you've been striving for. An empty heart has been filled, an unknown love revealed, a chase suspended, a bad relationship upended, a friendship formulated and love reciprocated! Constant PDA has family and friends shaking their heads. As a matter of fact, friends begin wondering why you're not returning calls or hanging out anymore. It has now become harder to concentrate on anything other than spending time with your 'boo'!

If only this stage could be bottled up and opened if ever things soured a bit. Butterflies in the stomach and rapid heartbeats are some of the internal consequences of reaching this stage. Sometimes you pinch yourself wondering if this is actually real after all the time alone.

You know when people are at this stage, because you see them walking down the street, and instead of holding hands, they awkwardly try to walk and hug each other at the same time. They look like the couple that keeps falling down and eventually comes in last place during the three-legged race at the company get-together.

This feeling of love has been well worth the wait. It is everything you dreamed it would be. How exciting it is meeting someone who fits most, if not all, of the criteria on your checklist; and, who feels you meet all of theirs.

You hope this junior high-like euphoria never ends. Ideally, the movie ends here as you both ride off horseback toward the setting sun.

Soulmates! Is there even such a thing? Is there that one person whom you were destined or predestined to be with…forever? Soulmate insinuates a connection far beyond anything simply physical. It suggests something deeper than just sharing similar likes or dislikes. It teeters on the border of a deeper, spiritual connection. This, in turn, says that you get or understand each other at the innermost recesses of your being.

Why is it that some seem to find that proverbial soulmate and others don't? Ultimately, time will be the determining factor as to whether or not this phenomenon is manifest in your relationship. Too many times, I believe, a deep physical attraction can distort or commandeer one's emotions. But, who's to say that someone not deemed a soulmate in the beginning can't grow into that esteemed position!

Are you still searching for your soulmate…or, are you with that person now?

VII

(Uh oh! All good things...)
Appreciate

I will love, give love, real love,
I've been hurt before, and, yet, I still love-
Look, treasure or trash, you can't have it both ways,
Some good days, but, bad are most days-
If you want greener grass, then, jump that fence,
Or, else, appreciate all that is my essence-
I mean, think of all I've done and continue to do,
My heart was on display like a menu to you-
Have an entrée of love or a combination platter,
Whatever you desired of me, it didn't matter-
And, yet, you took advantage, took my love for granted,
With my heart, played around, in the ground you ran it-
Now, I'm stronger, so no longer will you neglect me,
Deny me, degrade me, nor, disrespect me-
For, your place in my heart, I can alleviate,
For, I'm sure there is another who can appreciate!

Inevitability! There are some things in life that are going to happen, regardless. On love's journey, it is inevitable that at some point or another, the relationship will be tested. The saying rings true that "what makes you laugh, can make you cry!" That thing that was adorable about your mate in the beginning can soon become an annoyance. Communication is not what it once was. Weight gain, snoring, kids, job loss and finances are just some of the issues that can present themselves, bringing about a negative change.

People deal with the stresses of a relationship in different ways. One of the more unfortunate recourses is to seek relief, if you will, outside the relationship. All of a sudden, someone who appears to be a stark contrast to the difficulties you are experiencing with your significant other becomes more appealing. Just the simple thought of venturing to apparent greener pastures can prove destructive to a relationship.

My humble advice, to anyone who has yet to take the ultimate step toward commitment in the form of marriage, is to be extremely mindful of the vows you utter and undertake at the ceremony.

Please do not take the 'for better or for worse' proclamation lightly. For there will be enough of both to go around. Make sure you fully understand all that the 'for worse' encompasses. Things will change, but, when they do, establishing a foundation of friendship and caring will aid you in being man or woman enough to see it through!

There are stories aplenty about couples who have endured for 30, 40, 50, even 60 years of marriage. So, it is possible. Just remember to bring your hard hat and lunch pail because it does take work. Also, keep in mind, what it took to bring you together, it's going to take to keep you together!

Do you appreciate your mate? Do you feel appreciated?

Chapter VIII

(The refresh button)
You, Me and Unity

Unity usually combines us mutually,
But, nowadays unity is not what it used to be-
A string unseen would connect our hearts,
Together, one unit with two moving parts-
If I started a statement, you were able to finish it,
And, nothing, save God, could ever diminish it-
But, yet, the indivisible began to divide,
Hearts going separate ways began to collide-
Gas is a substance that moves a car,
However, minus oil, it won't go far-
The same applies in our lives, we're gonna stall,
Without communication, unity, trust, and all-
So, tonight, let's reunite, repair that tie that binds us,
Surround our souls with things that remind us-
Of how it used to be when love was the key,
Communication, trust, and, of course, Unity!

So, as I alluded to previously, all relationships will encounter bumps in the road. Most, if not all, will reach the proverbial fork in the road. A decision must be made to either go separate ways or to stick in there and fight for what you have established. An open and honest dialogue serves as the ideal elixir to begin the process of reparation. All feelings must be disclosed and placed on the table during this stage of the journey. Nothing is too trivial or out of bounds if it is, in any way, contributory to the problem(s).

Your friend, that person you longed for, chased, and professed your love to, deserves nothing less than candid communication. If the relationship is salvageable, then, reflecting on both past highlights and lowlights, can lead to projecting what needs to be done in the future.

Talk about what made you laugh, or, talk about what made you cry. If true reconciliation is what you are both seeking, then, there is no need to hold anything back at this point. This does not mean that your mate has to agree with everything you disclose, but, hopefully that person is man or woman enough to understand your concerns.

What is/was the point of unity for you as a couple? Was it a common belief in God as the creator and head of your family? Do you both share a common humanitarian cause that is near and dear to your hearts that drew you together? Whatever that point of unity was/is for you, reflect on it! Remember what it is about that person that attracted you, that somehow got buried under late bill payments, who's dropping the kids off to school, or, whose turn to wash the dishes! Hit the refresh button and start anew. It's not too late!

Although there's an 'i' in unity, it will not exist without 'w' and 'e'!

Chapter IX

(Love of Self)
I Want To Live

Thoughts in my head sped to the wrong side,
I knew right then I was in for a long ride-
See, life is full of lumps, bumps and potholes,
But, would life crunch me up, like nachos-
There's no way I'd sit and just find out,
Hard life was winning, so, I called time out-
To regroup, reload, or quit,
I hit rock bottom in a bottomless pit-
Cooked like meat and life was a glutton,
To swallow me down, to life, it meant nothin'-
So, there I sat inside life's stomach,
But, I fought back, I made life vomit-
Me, back up to my original state,
For, I am the master of my fate!

(cont.)

'To be or not to be', you contemplate giving up,
Everyday you gotta hear how you're not living up-
To expectations that were set,
So, out of this world you try to jet-
Well, I can understand, but, that's not the answer,
I wrote these words to give you a chance to-
Evaluate, so you don't have to make,
A big mistake...wait-
Before you cut your wrist, please, listen to this,
There is no coming back when death is kissed-
You go and do something fatally drastic,
Now, there's your mom slumped over your casket-
Trying to figure out where she went wrong,
So, everybody...Live Long!

(cont.)

It's just food for thought I hope feeds your hunger,
Something to consider, contemplate, and ponder-
We all agonize over bills and money,
But, think about living in a third world country-
Where those people live in constant famine,
I betcha they'd be happy just to have a ham and-
Cheese sandwich, somehow they manage,
Get what they can and take advantage-
We can do the same in this thing called life,
So, drop the gun, put away the knife-
Come off the bridge, 'cause kids we need to go the length,
It's time we flexed our mental strength-
Live life to the fullest everyday,
And, don't try to leave until you're called away!

Love can't be simply compartmentalized to the confines of an intimate relationship. There are other aspects of love on this journey that must be considered. One of the most important of these is self-love. How can we truly expect to love others, if we don't truly love ourselves? Whether it is a result of condescending and disparaging remarks or actions perpetrated by others, or some other self-generated inferiority complex due to not meeting some societal standard, many people tend to struggle with loving themselves.

Bullying has become a despicable societal norm affecting our young people. Both physical and cyber-bullying have contributed to many lost souls taking their own lives. Humiliating someone based on sexual orientation, among other things, has contributed to emotional turmoil and depression in many of today's youth. The mental and emotional denigration of a young person, before he or she is able to lay down a solid foundation of self-love, has proven fatal in many a circumstance.

Suicide, however, is not relegated only to the young. Even adults are subject to severe and deep bouts of depression. Many struggle with self-worth based on a perceived lack of success in life.

Sometimes people allow others to set expectations for them, ones they may be unsuited to achieve. Moreover, there are those who do achieve a modicum of success and are unprepared to deal with it. A typical reaction by many is to seek escape in the form of drugs or alcohol. This, as we know, leads to a whole other set of demons with which to contend.

  Individually, in these situations, if we can not see the value and self-worth in ourselves, we must understand what those things mean to the Creator. We were uniquely and wonderfully made. When we truly understand and accept that, then, no one or nothing outside of our innermost sphere (our soul) should be able to tread where only we and the Creator exist. The recognition, acknowledgement and acceptance of the place where spirit and soul commune brings a sense of peace and self-love that no human can circumvent. Lacking self-love impacts self-confidence, which, in turn, is detrimental to any chance at finding true love.

Chapter X

(Love our Children)
Dead Beat Dad

You laid, gave and now misbehave,
But, this is no time for games to be played-
An extension of you has come to be,
And, all of the love shouldn't come from me-
Nevermind me, consider the seed,
That you planted, take for granted, please take heed-
This is no way for a child to be reared,
Like a runaway train, you've disappeared-
It was our choice, don't punish the child,
We knew the consequences of passion gone wild-
When you neglect, you reject a part of yourself,
A kid is not a memoir you place on the shelf-
Like some trophy you glance at every now and then,
Pat yourself on the back, remembering when-
No, a child is someone you must be involved with,
And, this problem we face can only be solved if-
You decide to be the man you pretended to be,
The night you laid down and made love to me!

Just to clear up any confusion, first and foremost, I had a former work colleague who asked if I could write something for her ex-boyfriend. I wrote this poem in the form of a greeting card and she sent it to him on their child's birthday. Nevertheless, in the previous chapter, we discussed self-love, or the lack thereof. Very often, this lack of self-love is created in the home. This is not to say or suggest that children reared in a two-parent home are immune to feeling invisible, unwanted or unloved. However, I believe the chances for the manifestation of these feelings are augmented when there is a single-parent environment; especially, if one parent is not involved in the child's life.

An unfortunate reality is that on this journey of love that we traveled up to this point, not all situations or relationships will end 'happily ever after'. Couples sometimes reach the point where it is believed that separation is the only solution. Usually, the African proverb that says "when the elephants go to war, it is the trees that suffer", is appropriate in these circumstances.

Now, that may not be word for word how that quote goes; however, the point should be well taken. When the parents are at odds, the child(ren) will suffer. Many children take this pain with them well into adulthood.

My intent is not to judge whether or not two people should remain together. My intent is to suggest that two people should work together for the betterment of the children. Personal feelings have to be set aside so that any child involved will feel loved by mother and father, if one or the other is not living in the home. The navigation through life is tough enough as it is for young people, without the easily correctable feeling of appearing unwanted by one parent or another. Children want, need and deserve time, not just a check!

Do you truly believe the children are our future?

Chapter XI

(A Motherly Love)
Hey Mom!

***She** overcame all stress, tribulation and strife,*
Worked her fingers to the bone everyday of her life-
So, I can have all I wanted when I was a kid,
And, I wanna pay her back for all she did-
Because she worked so very hard, we were never poor,
But, I feel she deserves so much more-
For mom, I wanna be a superstar,
So she can have a nice house and drive a big car-
And, not have to worry 'cause the bills are paid,
Just lay out by her pool, have it made in the shade-
Eat the finest foods, sip the best champagne,
Live a trouble-free life and never have to complain!

(cont.)

Nine *months of pregnancy, oh, what pain,*
What physical hurt and what a mental strain-
But, mom, she persevered, though the burden was large,
And, for me, it was free, all for no charge-
She never asked for anything in return,
Except, I stay in school, so I could learn-
Learn all the things she already knew,
Couldn't see it back then, but, now I do-
She tried to get it in my head, that life was hard,
Wanted me to be prepared from the very start-
And, everything she ever told me turned out to be true,
It might not be much mom, but, this poem's for you!

(cont.)

Pancakes *in the morning, for dinner, beef stew,*
She brought me back to health when I was out with the flu-
Was always in attendance at every ballgame,
And, on the back of her shirt, she cold sported my name-
Because I made her so proud, she called me number one,
Said, I was her shining star, so, she called me son-
But, even though I made her happy, I'm wearing a frown,
In many ways, I feel like I've let her down-
It wasn't always sun and fun, there were many rainy days,
But, nevertheless, I will love her always!

So, *don't wait too late, don't hesitate,*
To hug your mom, say you love her, tell her she's great-
It's the least you can do, if you ask me,
Share love, hugs, and then you'll see-
You'll see that you get along better with,
That mother of yours, because love's the only gift-
She will need, take heed to these words I rhyme,
And, much love to all the sweet mothers like mine!

This has been the most difficult chapter for me to write. It feels as though I spent countless hours staring at the blank page and blinking line trying to figure out what to say. My mom transitioned to Heaven on December 16, 2013! And, since then, my life has been like a blank Word document with a blinking line. Empty! Many times in life, I find myself not sure what to do. She was supposed to always be there. She was always there, until she wasn't.

It was mentioned previously that as children, our first encounter with love is in the home. I am well aware that for some people the father served this role. I am well aware that fathers are capable of fulfilling this role. My experience, and that of many others, was one in which the parental love we needed came by way of the mother. I was fortunate enough to have a mother, and grandmother, whose primary concern was that of the well-being of every member of the family.

Selfless! They put everybody else before themselves. My mom's home and heart for many years was the hub of the family. If ever there was a family issue or concern, she was aware and frequently consulted about it.

Even as she climbed the ladder professionally and became a well-respected member in the healthcare field (she had just finished coursework for her *PhD* at the time of her passing), you never felt as though she did not have time for you.

At one point, early in my life, I couldn't imagine loving anything or anyone more than my mom. That included the God that created her. I realize, now, how sacrilegious that was. It's just that at that time, when I wasn't as grounded in my faith as I am now, I responded to what I was able to see with my physical eyes.

I witnessed, firsthand, the love she had for me and my brothers, despite all of the challenges associated with raising five boys. I witnessed, firsthand, how she gave of herself to extended family and friends alike. It was difficult for me to see anything or anyone exemplifying love more than she did. Now, I understand better, but, for a long period of my life, I didn't.

A good mother offers her counsel regarding affairs of the heart. Then, when you opt not to follow her advice, she is there with a caring heart if things don't go the way you hoped. She never offers an "I told you so!" They care enough about you to allow you to make some mistakes, but, are always there to assist in putting the emotional pieces back together again. My mom wasn't perfect, but, she was perfect for me.

A good example set by a mother or father is central to successful navigation of love's journey. We can learn love in its most purest and unselfish sense from the way our parents love us. I take true solace in the fact that a few months prior to her passing, my mom cooked breakfast for me and her (breakfast was our favorite meal of the day) for the last time. After breakfast, at the kitchen table, she told me how proud she was of the man that I had become. Surely, she had to be aware of the major role she played in that.

After hearing those words from her, considering the circumstances they were uttered, there is now no one, or nothing, that can break down what she was so instrumental in building up within me.

Thank you, Mom! I love you for who you were to me! I will work feverishly to live a life worthy of His approval so that I may see you again…In Heaven!.

Chapter XII

(Agape Love)
Can You Forgive Me?

Dear God! Remember that time my brother lay hurt,
His life on the line and I went berserk-
And, I came to you like never before,
In tears, on bended knees, I swore-
That, if you saw fit, this time, to spare him,
Lift him up, heal and repair him-
I'd change my ways and commit to you,
You did, but, to this day, I forget to do-
All of the things I promised I would,
I'll ask, although I'm not sure I should-
Can you forgive me?
Many a night, drunk from that gin,
As my body tried to purge all that's within-
I promised to abstain if you'd stop the dry-heavin',
And, my word was bond, until the next weekend-
Whenever I'm sick, I'm quick to call you,
Sometimes I blame you whenever plans fall through-
I do not deserve your Grace and Mercy,
But, your word teaches that you won't desert me-
In fact, there is something I should always know,
Through your Son, you forgave me a long time ago!

I labored in writing this book on whether, or not, to place this chapter at the beginning or the end. I chose to place it at this juncture because every other step on this journey of love is enveloped in the love of God; or, at least they should be. There is no love like the love of God the Father, Agape Love!

How can anything or anyone surpass the love of the one who created it? His love knows no boundaries! His love is limitless! He gave His Son to be beaten and crucified because He so loved the people He created. He loved us, you and I, enough that He allowed His only begotten Son to die for **Our** sins!

Loving a potential mate, an ex-girlfriend or boyfriend, a child's absentee mother or father, your own mother or father, and loving yourself are all consequences of loving the Most High God Almighty! No matter where you are on love's journey, keeping Him first is paramount to the success of that particular stage. His love is not fickle. Even, if we are being corrected or reprimanded by God, His love for us remains consistent.

King David is one of the most well-known biblical figures. Few, in the Bible, committed more egregious mistakes, or, sins, than David. But God, the Omniscient One, loved David enough to search out his heart and uncover that he was truly after God's own heart. David was truly repentant of the sins he committed against God. God, who despises sin, loved David more than He hated his sins. He loves us more than He hates our sins. This is not a blank check to sin knowingly and recklessly; however, He is a forgiving and understanding God who is always aware of the true intentions of our hearts.

Thus, truthfully, this and every journey in our lives should begin and end with the name synonymous with love, Jesus Christ, as our guide! Not only is He the Wonderful Counselor, but, He is also the Ultimate Compass. His guidance, not only points us toward happiness, but, it also leads us to salvation and eternal life. Maintaining our focus on the Holy Guide, during the journey to love and through life, will ensure successful navigation to the desired destination! Amen.

MARY JOYCE MCKINNON

In loving memory...